Winning in Service Markets Series: Vol. 13

Building a World-Class Service Organization
(Assessment Tool)

Jochen Wirtz

WS Professional

NEW JERSEY · LONDON · SINGAPORE · BEIJING · SHANGHAI · HONG KONG · TAIPEI · CHENNAI · TOKYO

Published by

WS Professional, an imprint of
World Scientific Publishing Co. Pte. Ltd.
5 Toh Tuck Link, Singapore 596224
USA office: 27 Warren Street, Suite 401-402, Hackensack, NJ 07601
UK office: 57 Shelton Street, Covent Garden, London WC2H 9HE

For orders of individual copies, course adoptions, and bulk purchases: sales@wspc.com
For orders of individual chapters and customized course packs: sales@wspc.com
For adaptations or translation rights and permissions to reprint; rights@wspc.com

Winning in Service Markets Series — Vol. 13
BUILDING A WORLD CLASS SERVICE ORGANIZATION (ASSESSMENT TOOL)

Copyright © 2018 by Jochen Wirtz

ISBN 9781944659455 (pbk)
ISBN 9781944659479 (mobile book)

Desk Editor: Karimah Samsudin

Printed in Singapore

Dedication

To my past and future EMBA and Executive Program participants.

I have been teaching EMBA and Executive Programs for over
20 years. This Winning in Service Markets Series is dedicated to you, the
participants from these programs. You brought so much knowledge and
experience to the classroom, and this series synthesizes this learning for future
EMBA candidates and managers who want to know how to bring their service
organizations to the next level.

Preface

The main objective of this series is to cover the key aspects of services marketing and management, and that is based on sound academic research. Therefore, I used the globally leading text book I co-authored with Professor Christopher Lovelock (Title: *Services Marketing: People, Technology, Strategy*, 8th edition) as a base for this series, and adapted and rewrote it for managers. This is a unique approach.

This series aims to aims to bridge the all-too-frequent gap between cutting edge academic research and theory, and management practice. That is, it provides a strongly managerial perspective, yet is rooted in solid academic research, complemented by memorable frameworks.

In particular, creating and marketing value in today's increasingly service and knowledge-intensive economy requires an understanding of the powerful design and packaging of intangible benefits and products, high-quality service operations and customer information management processes, a pool of motivated and competent front-line employees, building and maintaining a loyal and profitable customer base, and the development and implementation of a coherent service strategy to transform these assets into improved business performance. This series aims to provide the knowledge required to deliver these.

Winning in Service Markets comprises of the following volume:

Vol 1:   Understanding Service Consumers
Vol 2:   Positioning Services in Competitive Markets
Vol 3:   Developing Service Products and Brands
Vol 4:   Pricing Services and Revenue Management
Vol 5:   Service Marketing Communications
Vol 6:   Designing Customer Service Processes
Vol 7:   Balancing Capacity and Demand in Service Operations
Vol 8:   Crafting the Service Environment
Vol 9:   Managing People for Service Advantage
Vol 10: Managing Customer Relationships and Building Loyalty
Vol 11: Designing Complaint Handling and Service Recovery Strategies
Vol 12: Service Quality and Productivity Management
Vol 13: Building A World-Class Service Organization

Contents

Introduction

Service leadership is not based on outstanding performance within a single dimension. Rather, it reflects excellence across multiple dimensions. *Building a World-Class Service Organisation* is the last book in the Winning in Service Markets series by services marketing expert Jochen Wirtz. This book provides a summary of how a world-class service organization looks like as well as an assessment tool to evaluate the organization within each of the three functional areas of marketing, operations, and human resources.

Building a World-Class Service Organization

Marketing is so basic that it cannot be considered a separate function… It is the whole business seen from the point of view of its final result, that is, from the customer's point of view. Concern and responsibility for marketing must, therefore, permeate all areas of the enterprise.

Peter Drucker,
Management consultant, educator, and author
Described as a founder of modern management

[T]he more short-term a company's focus becomes, the more likely the firm will be to engage in behavior that actually destroys value.

Don Peppers and Martha Rogers
Founding partners of Peppers & Rogers Group
A customer-centric management consulting firm

"Why is it so hard for so many to realize that winners are usually the ones who work harder, work longer, and as a result, perform better?" and "Big things are accomplished only through the perfection of minor details".

John Wooden
Legendary former UCLA Basketball Team Coach

INTRODUCTION

This volume provides a summary of how a world-class service organization looks like, which can be used as an assessment tool. Financial impact of being a service leader is also discussed and the volume concludes with a call to action on the readers' part!

CREATING A WORD CLASS SERVICE ORGANIZATION

How would one describe a breakthrough service organization? Based on our observations having worked in the field of services marketing for decades, we observed that a number of characteristics are necessary (but may not be sufficient) for becoming and remaining a breakthrough service organization. Next, we will analyze more comprehensively how firms can be categorized into four performance levels, and how they can then move up the performance ladder.

From Losers to Leaders: Four Levels of Service Performance

Service leadership is not based on outstanding performance within a single dimension. Rather, it reflects excellence across multiple dimensions. In an effort to capture this performance spectrum, we need to evaluate the organization within each of the three functional areas described earlier — marketing, operations, and human resources. Table 1 categorizes service performers into four levels: *loser*, *non-entity*, *professional*, and *leader*.[2] At each level, there is a brief description of a typical organization across 12 dimensions.

Under the marketing function, we look at the role of marketing, competitive appeal, customer profile and service quality. Under the operations function, we consider the role of operations, service delivery (front-stage), backstage operations, productivity, and introduction of new technologies. Finally, under the human resources function, we examine the role of HRM, the workforce, and frontline management. Obviously, there are overlaps between these dimensions and across functions. There may also be differences in the relative importance of some dimensions in different industries and across different delivery systems. For instance, human resource management tends to play a more prominent strategic role in high-contact services. The goal of this overall service performance framework is to generate insights into how service leaders perform so well and what needs to be changed in organizations that are not performing as well as they might.

Table 1 is a useful tool to perform an in-depth appraisal of a company in a specific industry, as a point of departure, modifying some of the elements to create a customized assessment tool.

Service Losers. These firms are at the bottom of the barrel from customer, employee, and managerial perspectives, and get failing grades in marketing, operations, and HRM. Customers patronize them for reasons other than performance, typically because there is no viable alternative, which is one reason why service losers continue to survive. Managers of such organizations may even see service delivery as a necessary evil. New technology is introduced only under duress, and the uncaring workforce is a negative constraint on performance.

Service Non-entities. Although their performance still leaves much to be desired, service nonentities have eliminated the worst features of losers. Non-entities are dominated by a traditional operations mindset, typically based on achieving cost savings through standardization. Their marketing strategies are unsophisticated, and the roles of human resources and operations might be summed up respectively by the philosophies "adequate is good enough" and "if it ain't broke, don't fix it". Managers may talk about improving quality and other goals, but are unable to set clear priorities to have a clear direction, nor gain the respect and commitment of their employees (Figure 1). Several such firms are often found competing in a lackluster fashion within a given marketplace, and you might have difficulty distinguishing one from the others. Periodic price discounts tend to be the primary means of trying to attract new customers.

Service Professionals. Service professionals are in a different league from non-entities and have a clear market positioning strategy. Customers within the target segments seek out these firms based on their sustained reputation for consistently meeting expectations. Marketing is sophisticated, using targeted communications and pricing based on value to the customer. Research is used to measure customer satisfaction and obtain ideas for service enhancement. Operations and marketing work together to introduce new delivery systems, and recognize the trade-off between productivity and customer-defined quality. There are explicit

Table 1: Four Levels of Service Performance Assessment Tool.

Marketing Function		
Level	**1. Loser**	**2. Nonentity**
Role of Marketing	• Tactical role only • Advertising and promotions lack focus • No involvement in product or pricing decision	• Uses mix of selling and mass communication, using simple segmentation strategy • Makes selective use of price discounts and promotions; conducts and tabulates basic satisfaction surveys
Competitive Appeal	• Customers patronize a firm for reasons other than performance	• Customers neither seek nor avoid the firm
Customer profile	• Unspecified • A mass market to be served at a minimum cost	• One or more segments whose basic needs are understood
Service Quality	• Highly variable, usually unsatisfactory. • Subservient to operations priorities	• Meets some customer expectations • Consistent on one or two key dimensions, but not all

Legend: Score each area from '1' to '4' depending on the performance level of the organization that is being assessed. Average the scores for each function, and then average the functions to obtain the total assessment score.

Marketing Function		
3. Professional	**4. Leader**	**Assessment Score**
• Has clear positioning strategy against competition • Uses focused communications with distinctive appeals to clarify promises and educate customers • Pricing is based on value • Monitors customer usage and operates loyalty programs • Uses a variety of research techniques to measure customer satisfaction and obtain ideas for service enhancements • Works with operations to introduce new delivery systems	• Innovative leader in chosen segments, known for marketing skills • Brands at product/process level • Conducts sophisticated analysis of relational databases as inputs to one-to-one marketing and proactive account management • Uses state-of-the-art research techniques • Uses concept testing, observation, and lead customers as inputs to new-product development • Close to operations/HR	
• Customers seek out the firm based on its sustained reputation for meeting customer expectations	• Company's name is synonymous with service excellence • Its ability to delight customers raises expectations to levels that competitors cannot meet	
• Groups of individuals whose variation in needs and value to the firm are clearly understood	• Individuals are selected and retained based on their future value to the firm, including their potential for new service opportunities and their ability to stimulate innovation	
• Consistently meets or exceeds customer expectations across multiple dimensions	• Raises customer expectations to new levels • Improves continuously	
Subtotal		

A score of "3.5 and above" indicates excellent performance; a score from "2.5. to 3.4" indicates good performance, a score from "1.5 to 2.4" indicates average to poor performance, and a score of "1.4 and lower" indicates very poor performance.

	Operations Function		
	1. Loser	**2. Nonentity**	
Role of Operations	• Reactive • Cost-oriented	• The principal line management function creates and delivers product • Focuses on standardization as key to productivity • Defines quality from internal perspective	
Service Delivery (front-stage)	• A necessary evil • Locations and schedules are unrelated to preferences of customers who are routinely ignored	• Sticklers for tradition; "If it ain't broke, don't fix it" • Tight rules for customers • Each step in delivery runs independently	
Back-stage Operations	• Divorced from front-stage operations • Cogs in a machine	• Contributes to individual front-stage delivery steps but organized separately • Unfamiliar with customers	
Productivity	• Undefined • Managers are punished for failing to stick within budget	• Based on standardization • Rewarded for keeping costs below budget	
Introduction of New Technology	• Late adopter, under duress, when necessary for survival	• Follows the crowd when justified by cost savings	

Legend: Score each area from '1' to '4' depending on the performance level of the organization that is being assessed. Average the scores for each function, and then average the functions to obtain the total assessment score.

Operations Function		
3. Professional	**4. Leader**	**Assessment Score**
• Plays a strategic role in competitive strategy • Recognizes a trade-off between productivity and customer-defined quality • Willing to outsource • Monitors competing operations for ideas, threats	• Recognized for innovation, focus, and excellence; an equal partner with marketing and HR management • Has in-house research capability and academic contacts • Continually experimenting	
• Driven by customer satisfaction, not tradition • Willing to customize, embrace new approaches • Emphasis on speed, convenience, and comfort	• Delivery is a seamless process organized around the customer • Employees know whom they are serving • Focuses on continuous improvement	
• Process is explicitly linked to front-stage activities • Sees role as serving "internal customers" who, in turn, serve external customers	• Closely integrated with front-stage delivery, even when geographically far apart • Understands how own role relates to the overall process of serving external customers • Continuing dialog	
• Focuses on re-engineering backstage processes • Avoids productivity improvements that will degrade customers' service experience • Continually refining processes for efficiency	• Understands the concept of return on quality • Actively seeks customer involvement in productivity improvement • Ongoing testing of new processes and technologies	
• An early adopter when IT promises to enhance service for customers and provide a competitive edge	• Works with technology leaders to develop new applications that create first-mover advantage • Seeks to perform at levels competitors cannot match	
	Subtotal	

A score of "3.5 and above" indicates excellent performance; a score from "2.5. to 3.4" indicates good performance, a score from "1.5 to 2.4" indicates average to poor performance, and a score of "1.4 and lower" indicates very poor performance.

Human Resources Function			
Level	**1. Loser**	**2. Nonentity**	
Role of Human Resources	• Supplies low-cost employees who meet minimum skill requirements for the job	• Recruits and trains employees who can perform competently	
Workforce	• Negative constraints: poor performers, do not care, disloyal	• Adequate resources, follows procedures but uninspired • Turnover often high	
Frontline Management	• Controls workers	• Controls the process	

Legend: Score each area from '1' to '4' depending on the performance level of the organization that is being assessed. Average the scores for each function, and then average the functions to obtain the total assessment score.

Human Resources Function		
3. Professional	**4. Leader**	**Assessment Score**
• Invests in selective recruiting, ongoing training • Keeps close to employees, promotes upward mobility • Strives to enhance the quality of working life	• Sees the quality of employees as a strategic advantage • The firm is recognized as outstanding place to work • HR helps top management to nurture culture	
• Listens to customers • Coaches and facilitates workers		
	Subtotal	
	Overall Total	

A score of "3.5 and above" indicates excellent performance; a score from "2.5. to 3.4" indicates good performance, a score from "1.5 to 2.4" indicates average to poor performance, and a score of "1.4 and lower" indicates very poor performance.

Note: This framework was inspired by, and expands upon, work in service operations management by Richard Chase and Robert Hayes.

Figure 1: Dilbert's boss loses focus — and his audience.

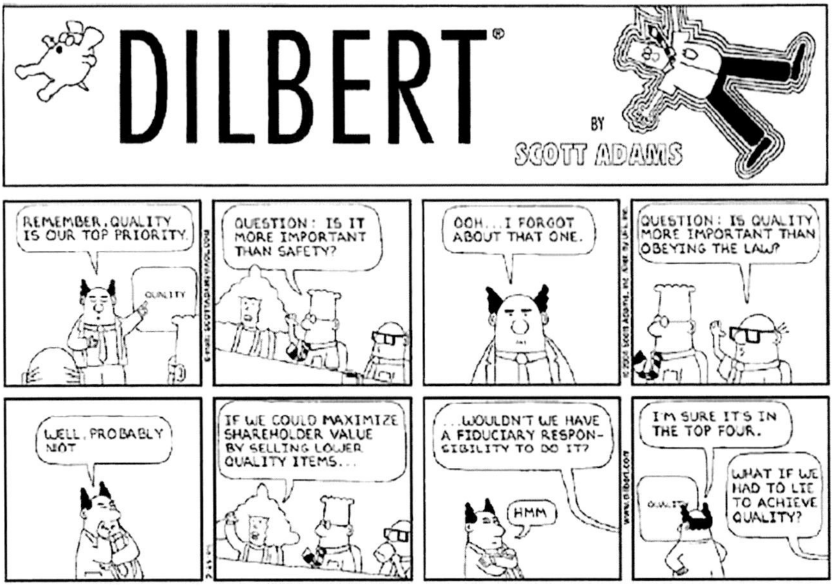

links between backstage and front-stage activities, and the firm has a much more proactive, investment-oriented approach to HRM than is found among nonentities.

Service Leaders. These organizations are breakthrough service organizations, world-class service leaders, and are the *crème de la crème* of their respective industries. Where service professionals are good, service leaders are outstanding. When we think of service leaders, we think of Amazon, McKinsey, Ritz Carlton, Southwest Airlines, Starbucks, and Zappos. Their company names are synonymous with service excellence and the ability to delight customers. Service leaders are recognized for their innovation in each functional area of management as well as for their superior internal communications and coordination among these three functions, often the result of a relatively flat organizational structure and the extensive use of teams. As a result, service delivery is a seamless process organized around the customer.

Marketing efforts by service leaders make extensive use of customer relationship management (CRM) systems that offer strategic insights about customers, who are often addressed on a one-to-one basis. Concept

Figure 2: Creating an outstanding work environment attracts and retains the best people.

testing, observation, and contacts with lead customers are employed in the development of new, breakthrough services that respond to previously unrecognized needs. Operations specialists work with technology leaders around the world to develop new applications that will create a first mover advantage, and enable the firm to perform at levels that competitors cannot hope to reach for a long time to come. Senior executives see quality of employees as a strategic advantage. HRM works on building and maintaining a service-oriented culture and creating an outstanding working environment that simplifies the task of attracting and retaining the best people (Figure 2).[3] The employees themselves are committed to the firm's values and goals. Because they are engaged, empowered, and quick to embrace change, they are an ongoing source of new ideas and they continuously drive improvement.

Moving to a Higher Level of Performance

Almost all companies want to be service leaders. We want to win our customers' loyalty and we want our customers to say good things about us. If we can achieve these objectives, we will increase our market share, our shareholder value, and our share of community goodwill. These are powerful reasons for moving to a higher performance level.[4] This view is becoming widely accepted, and in most markets we can find companies moving up the performance ladder through conscious efforts to improve and coordinate their marketing, operations, and HRM functions, in a bid to establish more favorable competitive positions and better satisfy their customers.

It requires human leaders at all levels of an organization to take a service firm in the right direction, set the right strategic priorities, and ensure the relevant strategies are implemented throughout the organization. And the various chapters throughout this book discuss exactly how it can be done through various tools, concepts, and theories.

CUSTOMER SATISFACTION AND CORPORATE PERFORMANCE

The philosophy of this series has been all about customer centricity and creating value for customers as a long-term core strategy. This perspective permeates many of the key concepts and models you have learned in this series, including the Service-Profit Chain, Cycle of Success, Service Talent Cycle, Wheel of Loyalty, and the Gaps Model. We therefore feel it is fitting to present another piece of evidence that long-term perspective and customer centricity will pay off financially.

There is convincing evidence of strategic links between the level of customer satisfaction with a firm's service offerings and overall firm performance. Researchers from the University of Michigan found that on average, every 1% increase in customer satisfaction is associated with a 2.4% increase in a firm's return on investment (ROI).[5] Analysis of companies' scores on the American Customer Satisfaction Index (ACSI) shows that, on average, among publicly traded firms, a 5% change in the ACSI score is associated with a 19% change in the market value of common equity.[6] In other words, by creating more value for the customer, as measured by increased satisfaction, the firm creates more value for its owners (*Service Insights 1*).

SERVICE INSIGHTS 1
Customer Satisfaction and Wall Street:
High Returns and Low Risk!

Does a firm's customer satisfaction levels have anything to do with its stock price? This was the research question Claes Fornell and his colleagues wanted to answer. More specifically, they examined whether investments in customer satisfaction led to excess stock returns (Figure 3), and if so, whether these returns were associated with higher risks as would be predicted by finance theory.

The researchers built two stock portfolios, one hypothetical back-dated portfolio and a real-world portfolio that tracked stock market performance in real time over several years. Both portfolios only consisted firms that did well in terms of their customer satisfaction ratings, as measured by the American Customer Satisfaction Index (ACSI).

The ACSI-based portfolios were rebalanced once a year on the day when the annual ACSI results were announced. Only firms in the top 20% in terms of customer satisfaction ratings were included (firms were either retained if they already were in the top 20% last year, or firms that improved their satisfaction ranking into the top 20% were added to the portfolio). Firms that fell below the 20% cut-off were sold. The return and risk of both portfolios were measured and their risk-adjusted returns were then compared to broad market indices such as the S&P 500 and NASDAQ.

Their findings are striking for managers and investors alike! Fornell and his colleagues discovered that the ACSI-based portfolios generated significantly higher risk-adjusted returns than their market benchmark indices and outperformed the market. Changes in the ACSI ratings of individual firms were significantly related to their future stock price movement, and as another study showed, even CEO compensation.[7]

However, simply publishing the latest data on the ACSI index did not immediately move share prices as efficient market theory would have predicted. Instead, share prices seemed to adjust slowly over time as firms published other results (perhaps earnings data or other 'hard' facts which may lag behind changes in customer satisfaction). A recent study in a retail context confirmed this time lag, whereby increases in customer satisfaction were shown to lag operational improvements, and profits lagged increases in customer satisfaction. Therefore, becoming a service champion requires a longer term perspective.[8]

The conclusion is that acting faster than the market to

Figure 3: Can customer satisfaction data help to outperform the market?

changes in the ACSI index generated excess stock returns. This finding represents a stock market imperfection, but it is consistent with research in marketing, which holds that satisfied customers improve the level and the stability of cash flow.

In a later study, Lerzan Aksoy and her colleagues built on these findings and also confirmed that a portfolio based on ACSI data outperformed the S&P 500 index over a 10-year period and delivered risk-adjusted abnormal returns.

For marketing managers, the findings of both studies confirm that investments (or "expenses") into managing customer relationships and the cash flows they produce are fundamental to the firm's, and therefore shareholders' value creation.

Although the results are convincing, care must be taken while exploiting this apparent market inefficiency and investing in firms that show high increases in customer satisfaction in future ACSI releases as the efficient markets learn fast. It is evident from the movement of stock prices as a response of future ACSI releases. For more details about ACSI, visit www.theacsi.org.

Sources: Claes Fornell, Sunil Mithas, Forrest V. Morgeson III, and M.S. Krishnan, "Customer Satisfaction and Stock Prices: High Returns, Low Risk," *Journal of Marketing*, Vol. 70, January 2006, pp. 3–14. Lerzan Aksoy, Bruce Cooil, Christopher Groening, Timothy L. Keiningham, and Atakan Yalçin, "The Long-Term Stock Market Valuation of Customer Satisfaction," *Journal of Marketing*, Vol. 72, no. 4 (2008): 105–122.

CONCLUSION

Transforming an organization and maintaining service leadership is no easy task for even the most gifted leader. I hope that having worked through this series will help you to become a more effective marketer and leader in any service organization. I also hope we not only managed to equip you with the necessary knowledge, understanding and insights, but also with the beliefs and attitudes about what propels a firm to service leadership. If this series has motivated and excited you to become a service champion yourself, I as author have achieved my objectives.

For further readings, see the Appendix, where some of my favorite books and resources on services marketing and management are listed. If you have feedback and suggestions on how to further improve this book, do contact me via www.JochenWirtz.com or sg.linkedin.com/in/jochenwirtz. I would love to hear from you!

I started each volume with inspirational quotes, and like to end this volume with a quote by Tony Robbins: "*It's not knowing what to do, it's doing what you know*". On this note, I wish you enjoyment, fulfillment, and success in applying what you have learned.

APPENDIX: FURTHER RESOURCES ON SERVICES MARKETING AND MANAGEMENT

Below is a list of useful books, websites, and resources which is not exhaustive, but provides a starting point for anyone who is interested in delving deeper into this exciting topic. I also list some earlier books as they are classics and are still highly relevant. I apologize should we have missed important sources and, if so, let me know and I will update the list in the next edition.

Books

- Janelle Barlow and Claus Moller (2008), *A Complaint is a Gift*, 2nd Ed. Berrett-Koehler Publishers.

- Jonah Berger (2013), *Contagious: Why Things Catch On*. Simon & Schuster.

- Leonard L. Berry and Kent D. Seltman (2008), *Management Lessons from Mayo Clinic: Inside One of the Most Admired Service Organizations*. McGraw-Hill.

- Sriram Dasu and Richard B. Chase (2013), *The Customer Service Solution: Managing Emotions, Trust, and Control to Win Your Customer's Business*. McGraw Hill.

- Thomas J. DeLong, John J. Gabarro and Robert J. Lees (2007), *When Professionals Have to Lead: A New Model for High Performance*. Harvard Business School Press.

- James A. Fitzsimmons and Mona J. Fitzsimmons (2013), *Service Management: Operations, Strategy, Information Technology*, 8th Ed. McGraw–Hill.

- Frances Frei and Anne Morriss (2012), *Uncommon Service: How to Win by Putting Customers at the Core of Your Business*. Harvard Business Review Press.

- James L. Heskett, W. Earl Sasser, Jr. and Joe Wheeler (2008), *The Ownership Quotient*. Harvard Business School Press.

- Tony Hsieh (2013), *Delivering Happiness: A Path to Profits, Passion, and Purpose*. Grand Central Publishing.

- Robert Johnston, Graham Clark, and Michael Shulver (2012), *Service Operations Management: Improving Service Delivery*, 4th Ed. Prentice Hall.

- Robert F. Lusch and Stephen L. Vargo (2014), *Service-Dominant Logic: Premises, Perspectives, Possibilities*. Cambridge University Press.

- Richard L. Oliver (2010), *Satisfaction: A Behavioral Perspective on the Consumer*, 2nd Ed. M.E. Sharpe.

- Roland T. Rust, Katherine N. Lemon and Das Narayandas (2005), *Customer Equity Management*. Pearson Prentice Hall.

- Valarie A. Zeithaml, Mary Jo Bitner and Dwayne D. Gremler (2012), *Services Marketing: Integrating Customer Focus Across the Firm*, 6th Ed. McGraw–Hill.

- Laurie Young (2005), *Marketing the Professional Service Firm*. John Wiley & Sons.

Leading Service Research Centers and Their Websites

- The Cambridge Service Alliance at the University of Cambridge in England (http://cambridgeservicealliance.eng.cam.ac.uk).

- The Center for Excellence in Service of Robert H. Smith School of Business at University of Maryland (www.rhsmith.umd.edu/ces).

- The Center for Services Leadership at the W. P. Carey School of Business at Arizona State University (http://wpcarey.asu.edu/csl).

- The Institute of Service Excellence at the Singapore Management University (http://ises.smu.edu.sg).

- The Service Research Center at Karlstad University in Sweden (www.ctf.kau.se).

Listing of Other Resources

There are a number of websites and blogs of firms with in-depth service expertise and leading service providers, but blogs and their contents and focus change fast. I therefore list a few companies you can follow on LinkedIn or search for their websites and blogs;

- Firms: Accenture, Disney Institute, Forrester, McKinsey & Company, Salesforce.com, UP! Your Service College.[9]

- For a listing of leading service-related blogs see: *50 Customer Experience Blogs You Should Be Reading*, available at http://www.ngdata.com/50-customer-experience-blogs-you-should-be-reading.

- Service design and innovation uses many different tools and methods originating from various disciplines. Several websites provide further resources, e.g. ServiceDesignTools.org and ServiceDesignThinking.com.

SUMMARY

1. Four Levels of Service Performance

There are four levels of service performance, and only the last two follow the key learnings from this book:

- *Service losers*: They are poor performers in marketing, operations, and HRM. Service losers survive because monopoly situations give customers little choice but to buy from them.

- *Service non-entities*: Their performance leaves much to be desired, but they have eliminated the worst features of losers.

- *Service professionals*: They have a clear market position, and customers in target segments seek them out based on their sustained reputation for meeting expectations. They are solid performers in marketing, operations, and HR, and the functions are tightly integrated.

- *Service leaders*: They are the breakthrough service champions, the crème de la crème of their respective industries. Their company names are synonymous with service excellence and an ability to delight customers.

Table 1 shows the contrast in the description and actions of a service leader against professionals, non-entities, and losers along the three functional areas. Service leadership requires high performance across a number of dimensions, including their sophistication of marketing, managing, and motivating employees, and continuously improving service quality and productivity.

2. Human Leaders

It requires human leaders at all levels of an organization to take a service firm in the right direction, and ensure that the right tools and relevant strategies are implemented throughout the organization.

3. Long-term Perspective and Customer Centricity

A service leader's adoption of a long-term perspective and customer centricity pays off financially. There is solid empirical evidence that high customer satisfaction (compared to an organization's peer group) leads to superior financial returns.

ENDNOTES

1   Peter Drucker did not regard himself as a marketer, yet his writing has had profound impact on the marketing field and discipline. The opening quote is discussed further in: Frederick E. Webster Jr., "Marketing IS management: The wisdom of Peter Drucker," *Journal of the Academy of Marketing Science,* Vol. 37, No. 1 (2009): 20–27.

2   The operations perspective was originally developed by: Richard B. Chase and Robert H. Hayes, "Beefing Up Operations in Service Firms," *Sloan Management Review,* Fall 1991, pp. 15–26. The framework shown in this chapter has been significantly extended to incorporate the marketing and HR functions, and has been updated.

3   Claudia H. Deutsch, "Management: Companies Scramble to Fill Shoes at the Top," *nytimes.com,* 1 November 2000.

4   This book provides you with the tools and knowledge to develop a winning services marketing strategy and with key tools to shape HR, operations and IT towards service excellence. In addition, there are a number of audit tools and checklists you can consult to assess a service organization. They include:

James L. Heskett, W. Earl Sasser, and Leonard A. Schlesinger (2003), *The Value Profit Chain: Treat Employees Like Customers and Customers Like Employees.* Free Press, NY: New York, Appendix B: The Value Profit Chain Audit, pp. 318–337.

James L. Heskett, W. Earl Sasser, and Joe Wheeler (2008), *The Ownership Quotient: Putting the Service Profit Chain to Work for Unbeatable Competitive Advantage.* Boston, Massachusetts: Harvard Business Press, Appendix B: Audition Ownership, pp. 193–203.

The European Foundation for Quality Management (EFQM) has detailed assessment sheets for all dimensions of the EFQM Model. They can be downloaded free-of-charge from http://www.efqm.org/efqm-model/efqm-model-in-action-0.

5   Eugene W. Anderson and Vikas Mittal, "Strengthening the Satisfaction-Profit Chain," *Journal of Service Research,* 3, November 2000, pp. 107–120.

6   Claes Fornell, Sunil Mithas, Forrest V. Morgeson III, and M.S. Krishnan, "Customer Satisfaction and Stock Prices: High Returns, Low Risk," *Journal of Marketing,* Vol. 70, January 2006, pp. 3–14.

7   A large-scale empirical study based on the ACSI showed that CEOs benefit if their firms outperform their peer group in terms of customer satisfaction in form of higher annual bonuses over and above what was explained by typical financial performance metrics and key control variables; see: Vincent O'Connel and Don O'Sullivan (2011), "The Impact of Customer Satisfaction on CEO Bonuses", *Journal of the Academy of Marketing Science,* Vol. 39, No. 6, pp. 828–845.

8   The authors estimated that a 20% increase in operational investments to improve service resulted in an immediate drop in operating profits, which only in the next year resulted in an increase in profit of twice the drop experienced in the year

of investment, see: Heiner Evanschitzky, Florian v. Wangenheim and Nancy V. Wünderlich (2012), "Perils of Managing the Service Profit Chain: The Role of Time Lags and Feedback Loops", *Journal of Retailing*, Vol. 88, No. 3, pp. 356–366.

9   Disclosure: Jochen Wirtz has a small equity stake in UP! Your Service College and was involved in early development and positioning of the college.

ABOUT THE AUTHOR

 **Jochen Wirtz** is Professor of Marketing and Vice Dean, Graduate Studies, at the National University of Singapore (NUS), and an international fellow of the Service Research Center at Karlstad University, Sweden. Furthermore, he is the founding director of the dual degree UCLA–NUS Executive MBA Program (ranked globally #6 in the Financial Times 2016 EMBA rankings) and international fellow of the Service Research Center at Karlstad University, Sweden, and Academic Scholar at the Cornell Institute for Healthy Futures (CIHF) at Cornell University, USA. Dr. Wirtz holds a PhD in services marketing from the London Business School and has worked in the field of services for over 25 years.

Professor Wirtz's research focuses on service marketing and has been published in over 200 academic articles, book chapters and industry reports. He is an author or co-author of more than 10 books, including *Services Marketing — People, Technology, Strategy* (8th edition) (World Scientific, 2016), co-authored with Professor Lovelock, which has become one of the world's leading services marketing text book that has been translated and adapted for more than 26 countries and regions, and with sales of some 800,000 copies.

In recognition of his excellence in teaching and research, Professor Wirtz has received more than 40 awards, including the prestigious Academy of Marketing Science (AMS) 2012 Outstanding Marketing Teacher Award (the highest recognition of teaching excellence of AMS globally), and the top university-level Outstanding Educator Award at NUS. He was also the winner of the inaugural Outstanding Service Researcher Award 2010, and the Best Practical Implications Award 2009, both by Emerald Group Publications.

Professor Wirtz was a banker and took the banking exam at Chamber of Commerce and Industry in Munich. He has since been an active management consultant, working with international consulting firms including Accenture, Arthur D. Little and KPMG, and major service firms in the areas of strategy, business development and customer feedback systems. He has also been involved in several start-ups including in Accellion (www.accellion.com), Angeloop (https://angeloop.co), TranscribeMe (www.transcribeme.com), and Up! Your Service (www.upyourservice.com).

Originally from Germany, Professor Wirtz spent seven years in London before moving to Asia. Today, he shuttles between Asia, the US and Europe. For further information, see www.JochenWirtz.com.

ACKNOWLEDGMENTS

First, I would like to thank my mentor, friend and co-author Professor Christopher Lovelock. Since first meeting in 1992, he has become a dear friend who has had significant influence on my thinking and development. We have worked together on a variety of projects, including cases, articles, conference papers, and several books. The Winning in Service Markets series is, in fact, derived from our best-selling textbook, *Services Marketing: People, Technology, Strategy*, 8th edition. I am eternally grateful to Christopher for his friendship and support.

Although it is impossible to mention everyone who has contributed in some way to this book through their research, their contributions and discussions at the many academic conferences where we have met, as collaborators on various research projects, and as friends who have always been ready to discuss, criticize, and provide feedback and suggestions. I particularly want to express my appreciation to the following: Tor Andreassen, Norwegian School of Management; John Bateson of Cass Business School; Leonard Berry of Texas A&M University; David Bowen of Thunderbird Graduate School of Management; Richard Chase of the University of Southern California; Jayanta Chatterjee of Indian Institute of Technology at Kanpur, India; James Heskett, Earl Sasser and Leonard Schlesinger, all of Harvard Business School; Bo Edvardsson of University of Karlstad; Pierre Eiglier of Université d'Aix-Marseille III; Michael Ehret of Nottingham Trent University; Raymond Fisk of the Texas State University; Christian Grönroos of the Swedish School of Economics in Finland; Miguel Angelo Hemzo, Universidade de São Paulo, Brazil; Irene Ng of University of Warwick; Jay Kandampully of Ohio State University; Ron Kaufman of UP! Your Service; Sheryl Kimes of Cornell University; Tim Keiningham of Rockbridge Associate; Jos Lemmink of Maastricht University; Xiongwen Lu of Fudan University, China; Paul Maglio of University of California, Merced, USA; Anna Mattila of Pennsylvania State University; Ulrich Orth of Kiel University; Chiara Orsingher of University of Bologna; A. "Parsu" Parasuraman of University of Miami; Paul Patterson of the University of New South Wales, Australia; Anat Rafaeli of Technion-Israeli Institute of Technology, Roland Rust of the University of Maryland; Benjamin Schneider formerly of the University of Maryland; Jim Spohrer of IBM; Javier Reynoso of Tec de Monterrey, Mexico; Christopher Tang of UCLA; Rodoula Tsiotsou of University of Macedonia; and Valarie Zeithaml of the University of North Carolina.

Finally, I'd like to thank you, the reader of this book, for your interest in this exciting and fast-evolving field of services management and marketing. If you have any feedback, please contact me via www. JochenWirtz.com. I'd love to hear from you!

Winning in Service Markets Series

Series Editor: Jochen Wirtz *(National University of Singapore, Singapore)*

The Winning in Service Markets Series covers the key aspects of services marketing and management based on sound academic evidence and knowledge. The books in this series is written by services marketing expert Jochen Wirtz, author of globally leading textbook for Services Marketing. Each book in the series covers different themes in the study of services marketing and management, is accessible, practical and presented in an easy-to-read format for busy practitioners and eMBA students.

Published:

*More information on this series can also be found at:
http://www.worldscientific.com/series/wsms

Services Marketing is available for various audiences:

Essentials of Services Marketing
Published by Pearson Education

Services Marketing: People, Technology, Strategy

Winning in Service Markets: Success Through People, Technology Strategy

---

Suitable for:
- Polytechnic Students
- Undergraduate Students

Suitable for:
- Advanced Undergraduate Students
- Master's-Level/MBA Students

Suitable for:
- Executive Program/EMBA Participants
- Practitioners/Senior Management

Available in the following formats:
- Paperback
- E-book

Available in the following formats:
- Hardcover
- Paperback
- E-book
- Bundle of Paperback & E-book

Available in the following formats:
- Hardcover
- Paperback
- E-book
- Bundle of Paperback & E-book

Services Marketing Series
- The content in terms of core theory, models and frameworks is largely the same across these publications. However, they are presented and designed to fit their particular target audiences.
- Services Marketing is available in some 26 languages and adaptations for key markets around the world.

Winning in Service Markets Series

Key chapters of Winning in Service Markets are available as stand-alone publications in e-book and paperback:
- Vol. 1: Understanding Service Consumers
- Vol. 2: Positioning Services in Competitive Markets
- Vol. 3: Developing Service Products & Brands
- Vol. 4: Pricing Services and Revenue Management
- Vol. 5: Service Marketing Communications
- Vol. 6: Designing Customer Service Processes
- Vol. 7: Balancing Capacity and Demand in Service Operations
- Vol. 8: Crafting the Service Environment
- Vol. 9: Managing People for Service Advantage
- Vol. 10: Managing Customer Relationships and Building Loyalty
- Vol. 11: Designing Complaint Handling and Service Recovery Strategies
- Vol. 12: Service Quality and Productivity Management
- Vol. 13: Building a World Class Service Organization

Contact
- For orders of individual copies, course adoptions, bulk purchases: sales@wspc.com
- For orders for individual chapters, customized course packs: sales@wspc.com
- For adaptions or translation rights, permissions to reprint: rights@wspc.com
- For further information see: www.JochenWirtz.com
- For questions regarding contents: Jochen Wirtz, jochen@nus.edu.sg.

Made in United States
Orlando, FL
09 December 2025

74188630R00021